The Ultimate Beginner Series®

ELECTRIC GUITAR BASICS

Revised Edition

Keith Wyatt

Alfred Music Publishing Co., Inc.
P.O. Box 10003
Van Nuys, CA 91410-0003
alfred.com

ISBN-10: 0-7390-8198-5 (Book & CD)
ISBN-13: 978-0-7390-8198-3 (Book & CD)

ISBN-10: 0-7390-8205-1 (Book, CD & DVD)
ISBN-13: 978-0-7390-8205-8 (Book, CD & DVD)

ISBN-10: 0-7579-8163-1 (DVD)
ISBN-13: 978-0-7579-8163-0 (DVD)

Cover photographs:
Guitar courtesy of Fender Musical Instruments Corporation.
Blue energy © iStockphoto.com / Raycat

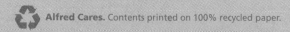

Contents

Section One: The Basics

PARTS OF THE GUITAR

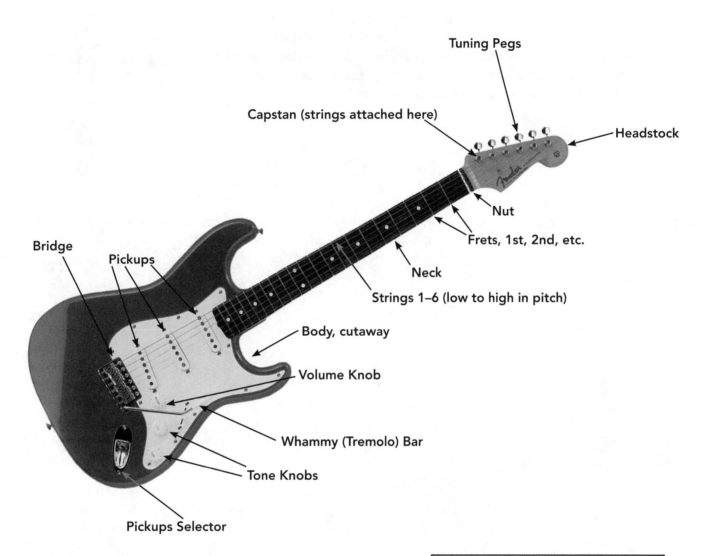

Tuning Pegs

Capstan (strings attached here)

Headstock

Nut

Frets, 1st, 2nd, etc.

Bridge

Pickups

Neck

Strings 1–6 (low to high in pitch)

Body, cutaway

Volume Knob

Whammy (Tremolo) Bar

Tone Knobs

Pickups Selector

Track 1 **INTRO SONG**

Track 2 **TUNING NOTES**

THE THREE BASIC GUITAR TYPES Track 3

THE NYLON-STRING ACOUSTIC (CLASSIC GUITAR)

The nylon string acoustic guitar has a nice mellow tone and has several advantages for beginners. The strings are much easier to press to the fretboard so they don't cut into your fingers the way steel strings do. Also, the neck is wider than on a typical steel string guitar, which makes fingering chords a little easier. The classic guitar is perfectly suited to intimate, unaccompanied guitar performances.

THE STEEL-STRING ACOUSTIC

The steel string acoustic guitar is perhaps the most versatile and common guitar type. Although it is a little bit harder to play than the nylon string guitar, the steel string acoustic has a loud, bright, ringing tone that clearly projects to the listener. This guitar is excellent for backing a singer.

The Electric Guitar

The electric guitar has come to dominate popular music. It is an extremely versatile instrument capable of producing everything from mellow jazz tones and biting funk riffs to the screaming, over-the-top, dizzying pyrotechnics of rock's reigning guitar virtuosos.

STRINGS

Strings are available in three basic gauges: light, medium, and heavy. I suggest you begin with light or medium gauge strings.

PICKS

Picks come in many shapes, sizes, and thicknesses . For acoustic guitar, I recommend light to medium thickness. For electric, the thicker picks seem to work best. Experiment to find the size and shape you are most comfortable with.

TUNING METHODS Track 4

TUNING TO A KEYBOARD:

The six strings of a guitar can be tuned to a keyboard by matching the sound of each open guitar string to the keyboard notes as indicated in the diagram.

Note: You will hear the intonation better, and your guitar will stay in better tune, if you loosen the strings and tune them up to pitch rather than starting above the correct pitch and tuning down.

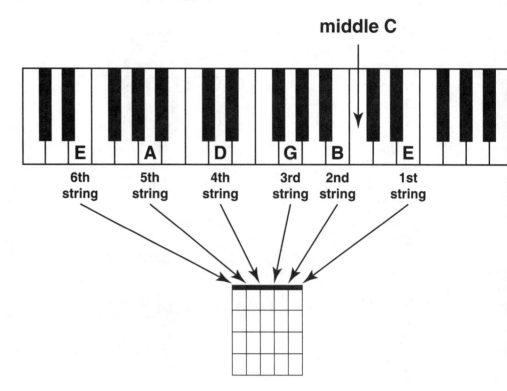

ELECTRONIC TUNERS:

Many brands of small, battery operated tuners are available. These are excellent for keeping your guitar in perfect tune and for developing your ear to hear intonation very accurately. Simply follow the instructions supplied with the electronic tuner.

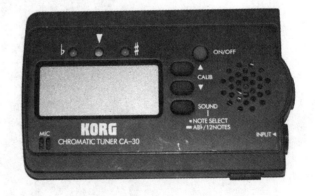

Tuning the Guitar to Itself—The "Fifth Fret" Method

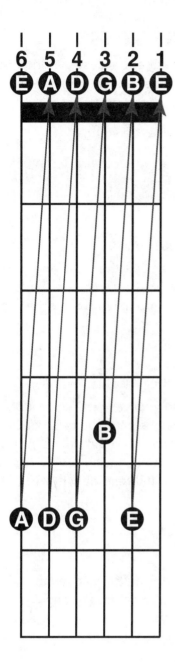

1. Either assume your 6th string "E" is in tune, or tune it to a piano or some other fixed-pitch instrument.

2. Depress the 6th string at the 5th fret. Play it and you will hear the note "A," which is the same as the 5th string played open. Turn the 5th string tuning key until the pitch of the open 5th string (A) matches that of the 6th string/5th fret (also A).

3. Depress the 5th string at the 5th fret. Play it and you will hear the note "D," which is the same as the 4th string played open. Turn the 4th string tuning key until the pitch of the open 4th string (D) matches that of the 5th string/5th fret (also D).

4. Depress the 4th string at the 5th fret. Play it and you will hear the note "G," which is the same as the 3rd string played open. Turn the 3rd string tuning key until the pitch of the open 3rd string (G) matches that of the 4th string/5th fret (also G).

5. Depress the 3rd string at the 4th fret (not the 5th fret as in the other strings). Play it and you will hear the note "B," which is the same as the 2nd string played open. Turn the 2nd string tuning key until the pitch of the open 2nd string (B) matches that of the 3rd string/4th fret (also B).

6. Depress the 2nd string at the 5th fret. Play it and you will hear the note "E," which is the same as the 1st string played open. Turn the 1st string tuning key until the pitch of the open 1st string (E) matches that of the 2nd string/5th fret (also E).

CHANGING STRINGS*

Eventually, whether because a string has broken on its own or is no longer "tunable" through repeated use, you will have to change your strings. Be prepared! Always keep the following in your guitar case:

1. A set of extra strings

2. A pair of wire cutters

3. A string winder

(All three items listed are available at your local music store.)

How to Change Strings

1. First, remove the old string. If the string has broken you will have to remove the "ball end" from the bridge and unwrap the other end from around the tuning peg.

2. Thread your new string through the hole in the bridge. On many electric guitars, you will have to turn the guitar over and thread the string through the holes in the back as shown here. On other electric guitars, the string will thread directly through a hole in the bridge.

3. Once the string has been threaded through the bridge, feed the other end through the hole in the tuning peg, making sure to leave some slack in the string.

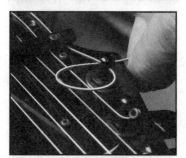

4. Bend the end slightly and, with your string winder, begin to tighten the string.

5. Trim the excess string off with your wire cutters.

*For information on changing acoustic or classic guitar strings, see "I Just Bought My First Guitar" (00-22705).

READING RHYTHM NOTATION

At the beginning of every song is a time signature. $\frac{4}{4}$ is the most common time signature:

$\frac{4}{4}$ = FOUR COUNTS TO A MEASURE
$\frac{4}{4}$ = A QUARTER NOTE RECEIVES ONE COUNT

The top number tells you how many counts per measure.
The bottom number tells you which kind of note receives one count.

The time value of a note is determined by three things:

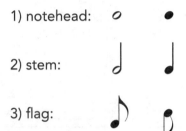

1) notehead:

2) stem:

3) flag:

This is a whole note. The notehead is open and has no stem. In $\frac{4}{4}$ time, a whole note receives 4 counts.

This is a half note. It has an open notehead and a stem. A half note receives two counts.

This is a quarter note. It has a solid notehead and a stem. A quarter note receives one count.

This is an eighth note. It has a solid notehead and a stem with a flag attached. An eighth note receives one half count.

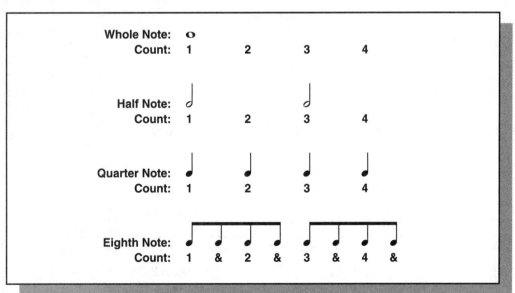

Rests indicate silence and there is a rest that corresponds to each note value. A whole rest ▬ lasts four beats, a half rest ▬ lasts two beats, a quarter rest 𝄽 lasts one beat, and an eighth note rest 𝄾 lasts one half count.

READING MUSIC NOTATION

Music is written on a *staff*. The staff consists of five lines and four spaces between the lines:

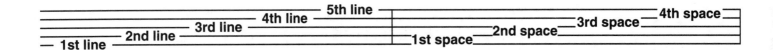

The names of the notes are the same as the first seven letters of the alphabet: A B C D E F G.

The notes are written in alphabetical order. The first (lowest) line is "E":

Notes can extend above and below the staff. When they do, *ledger lines* are added. Here is the approximate range of the guitar from the lowest note, open 6th string "E," to a "B" on the 1st string at the 17th fret.

The staff is divided into *measures* by *bar lines*. A heavy double bar line marks the end of the music.

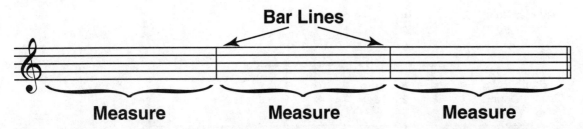

READING TABLATURE (TAB) AND FRETBOARD DIAGRAMS

Tablature (TAB) illustrates the location of notes on the neck of the guitar. This illustration compares the six strings of a guitar to the six lines of tablature.

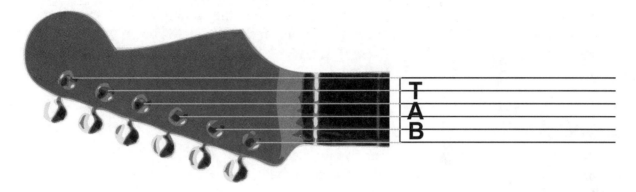

Notes are indicated by placing fret numbers on the strings. An "0" indicates an open string.

This tablature indicates to play the open, 1st and 3rd frets on the 1st string.

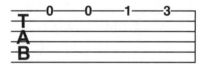

Tablature is usually used in conjunction with standard music notation. The rhythms and note names are indicated by the standard notation and the location of those notes on the guitar neck is indicated by the tablature.

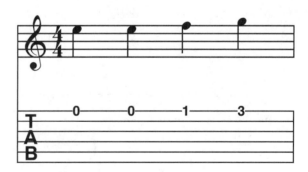

Chords are often indicated in *chord block diagrams.* The vertical lines represent the strings and the horizontal lines represent the frets. Scales are often indicated with guitar *fretboard diagrams.* Here the strings are horizontal and the frets are vertical. In this book, the *root*, or note name of the chord, is indicated by an open circle on the fretboard. For the chord below, all notes "C" are open circles.

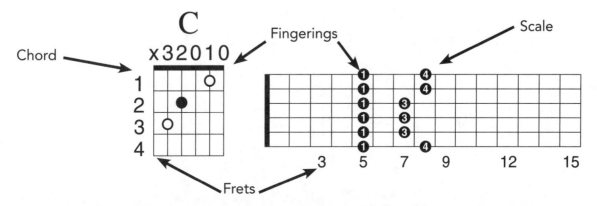

Section Two: Open-Position Chords

THE SIX BASIC OPEN-POSITION CHORDS

These are the most fundamental chords to all styles of guitar playing. "Open"-position chords contain open strings, which ring out loud and clear. The sound of a ringing open chord is probably the most identifiable guitar sound there is. Whether you play acoustic or electric guitar, these six chords will be some of the main chords you will use throughout your lifetime.

 Track 5

THE E MAJOR CHORD

The dots indicate which notes to play with your finger, the open circles indicate open strings and "x" indicates a string that should not be played. Play the E chord. Make sure you get a clear sound without any buzzing or muffled notes. Your fingertips should be placed just behind the fret—not on top of it or too far behind it. Also, the fingertips should be perpendicular to the fingerboard; if they lean at an angle they will interfere with the other strings and prevent them from ringing.

> ♯ = *Sharp*. A sharp sign indicates the note is played one fret higher than its *natural* position.

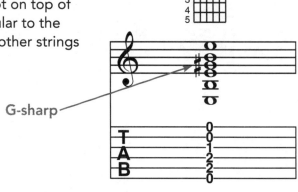

G-sharp

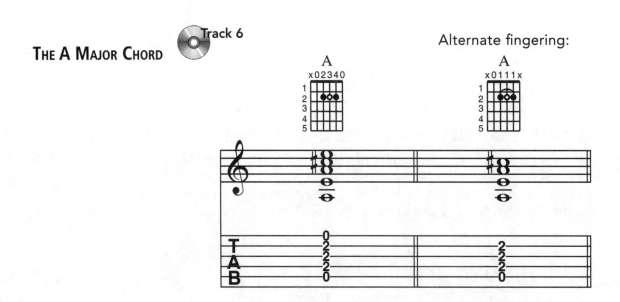 Track 6

THE A MAJOR CHORD

Alternate fingering:

Notice that in the alternate fingering there is no 1st string E. This is OK; it's still an A chord.

THE D MAJOR CHORD   Track 7

The D chord uses just the top four strings. Play the chord making sure you can get a good clear, ringing tone.

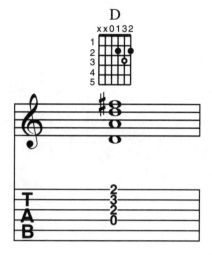

STRUMMING

Relax your left hand and strum with a constant down-up motion from your wrist. Strike the strings evenly with both the down-strum and, as your hand returns to playing position, with the up-strum. Down-strums are indicated with this symbol: ⊓. Up-strums are indicated with this symbol: V.

Listen to the recording and when you're ready, play along.

EXAMPLE I: FIRST STRUMMING PATTERN
Track 8

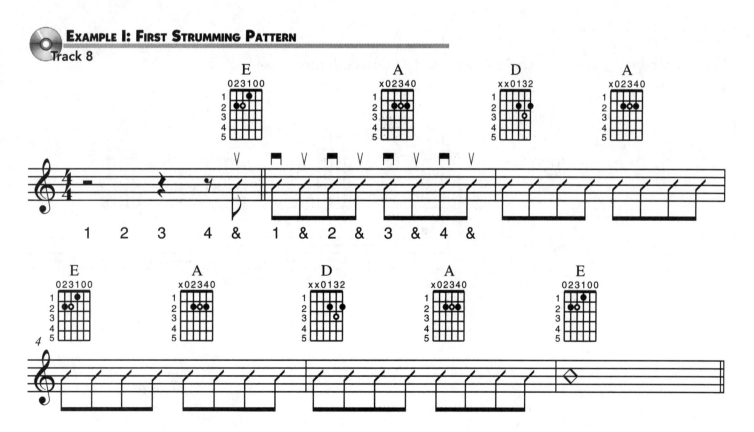

Track 9

G Major

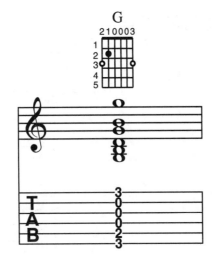

> **Tip:** In order to play this chord cleanly, it is essential that you play on your fingertips, holding your fingers perpendicular to the neck. Keeping your left-hand thumb down in the center of the neck will help keep your fingers in the best position to avoid interfering with the other strings.

EXAMPLE 2

Track 10

Now try combining the G chord with the D chord. Notice both chords use the same three fingers:

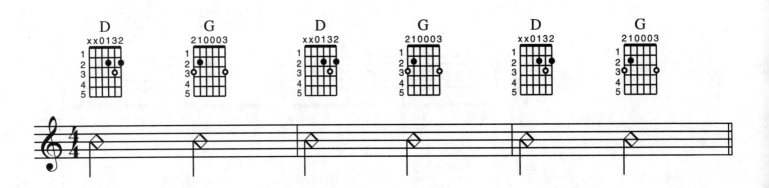

C Major

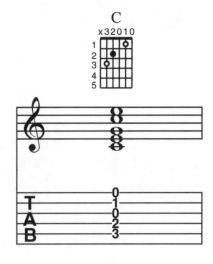

Remember: Hold your fingers perpendicular to the neck, making sure they touch only the strings they are playing and do not interfere with the other strings.

 **EXAMPLE 3**

Practice moving back and forth between the C and G chords.

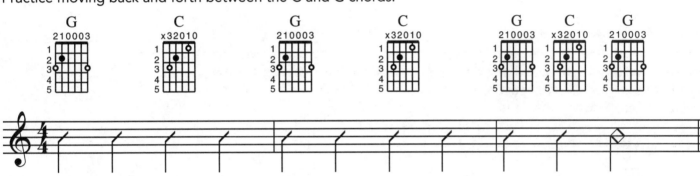

B7 Chord

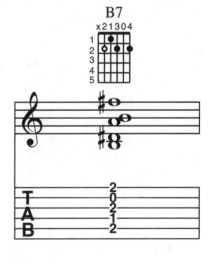

The G, D, C, and E chords each contain three different notes. The B7 is a four-note chord (B, D♯, F♯, A).

 EXAMPLE 4

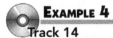

Now try this next example, which switches between the E and B7 chords.

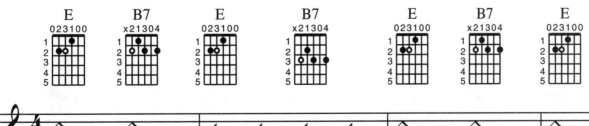

THE BLUES PROGRESSION (IN FOUR KEYS)

The blues *progression* (series of chords) is the most common chord progression. The typical blues progression is 12 measures long and uses the 1st, 4th and 5th chords of the *key* (a group of seven chords). To find the 1st, 4th, and 5th chords (usually indicated with Roman numerals: I, IV, and V) simply count up through the alphabet from the key note.

For Example:	Blues in the Key of "A":	A	B	C	D	E	F	G	A
		I			IV	V			
	Blues in the Key of "G":	G	A	B	C	D	E	F	G
		I			IV	V			
	Blues in the Key of "E":	E	F	G	A	B	C	D	E
		I			IV	V			
	Blues in the Key of "D":	D	E	F	G	A	B	C	D
		I			IV	V			

EXAMPLE 5: STRUM PATTERN A
Track 15.1

The next progression can be played with a variety of "strum" patterns. First try this simple "quarter-note" (one strum per beat) pattern. It can be played with either your pick, for a clear, bright sound; or your thumb, which gives it a darker, warmer sound. Listen to the recording to hear the difference.

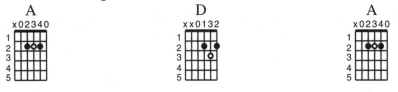

EXAMPLE 6: STRUM PATTERN B
Track 15.2

This next pattern uses both down- and up-stums of the pick. Your right hand should maintain a constant down-up motion, hitting the strings on all of the down-strums and on some of the up-strokes.

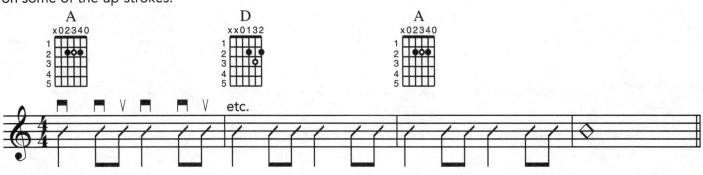

EXAMPLE 7
Track 16

This strumming example takes the blues progression through four keys: A, G, E, and D. It uses just the six chords you've learned so far: A, D, E, G, C and B7. Play along with the recording using the two rhythms you've just learned. When you're comfortable with the chord changes, try making up some rhythms of your own.

/ / / / = This kind of *slash notation* means to play any appropriate rhythm.

BLUES IN FOUR KEYS

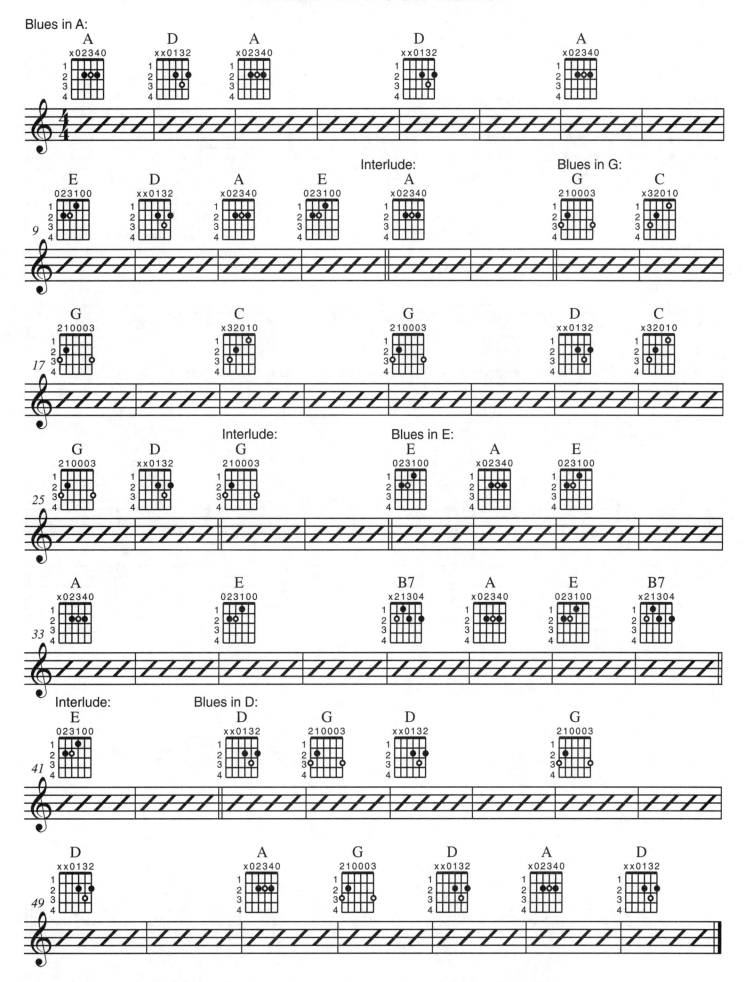

CHORD CATEGORIES

There are three categories of chords: Major, Minor and Dominant. With these three types of chords you can play basically any pop or rock song. You already know five basic open position major chords: E, D, C, A, and G.

Minor Chords: Minor chords differ from major chords by only one note: the 3rd. (To find the "3rd" count up three from the root, which is by definition the 1st note). By lowering the 3rd of any major chord one fret, the chord becomes a minor chord.

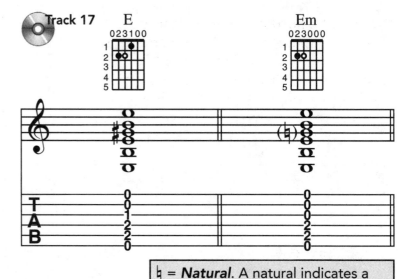

 **EXAMPLE 8**
Track 18

Play back and forth between the E and Em chords:

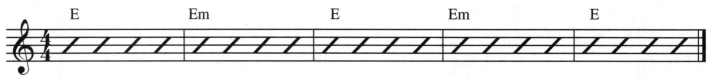

Notice again that the difference between the A and Am, and D and Dm chords is only one note (the 3rd).

♮ = **Natural.** A natural indicates a note is neither sharp nor flat.

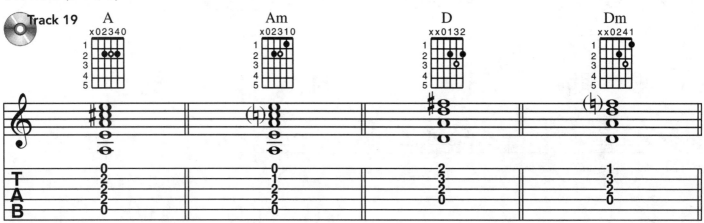

 **EXAMPLE 9**
Track 20

Play back and forth between the A and Am chords:

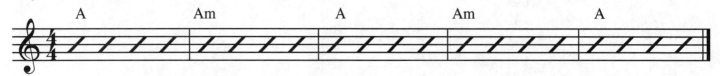

 **EXAMPLE 10**
Track 21

Play back and forth between the D and Dm chords:

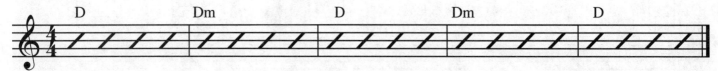

Dominant Chords: Dominant chords differ from major chords by the addition of one note: the 7th. To find the "7th," count up seven from the root (1). Adding the 7th to a major chord makes it a dominant 7th chord.

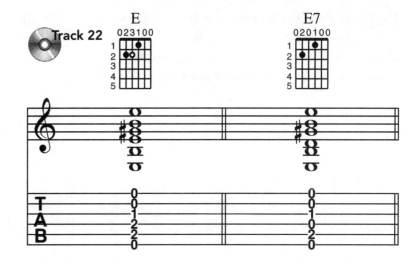

EXAMPLE II
Track 23

Play back and forth between the E and E7 chords. Listen closely to the difference in sound the one new note makes:

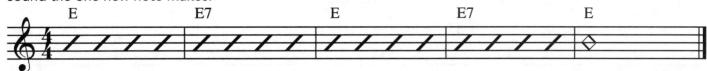

The difference between the A and A7, and D and D7 chords is again the addition of one note: the 7th.

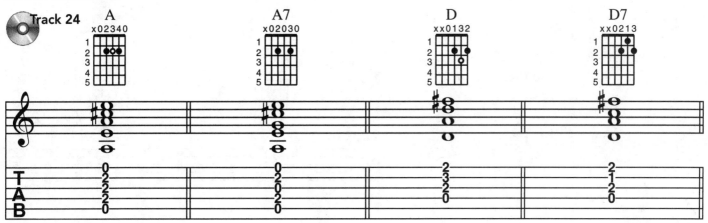

EXAMPLE 12
Track 25

Play back and forth between the A and A7 chords:

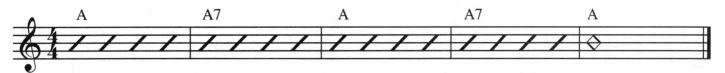

EXAMPLE 13
Track 26

Play back and forth between the D and D7 chords:

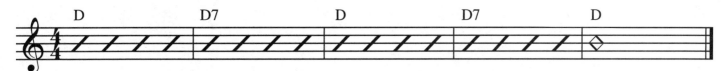

The open position G chord can be converted to a G7 chord as shown here. Try fingering the G chord with your 2nd, 3rd, and 4th fingers. This will make the change to G7 easier.

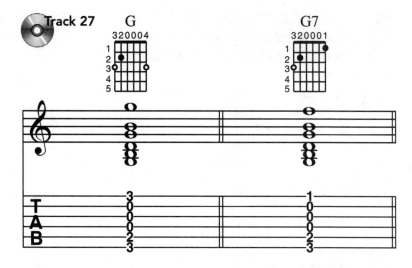

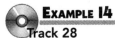

EXAMPLE 14
Track 28

Play back and forth between the G and G7 chords:

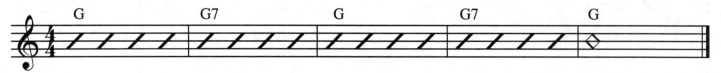

Now try converting the C to a C7. This is done by adding the 4th finger to the 3rd string.

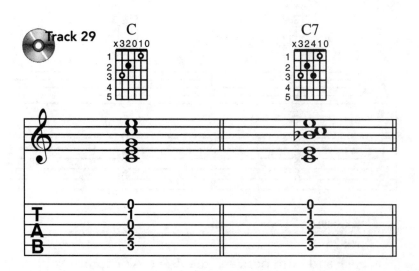

EXAMPLE 15
Track 30

Play back and forth between the C and C7 chords:

Section Three: Barre Chords

 Track 31   There are two types of barre chords: those with their root on the 6th string and those with their root on the 5th string. Before we learn the barre chords let's first learn the notes on those two strings.

This diagram shows the location of the natural (no sharps or flats) notes on the 6th string. It is useful to remember that there is a whole step (two frets) between all adjacent natural notes except for "E–F" and "B–C," which are separated by a half step (one fret).

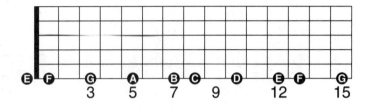

Here are the notes and tablature for the notes on the "E" string. Play these notes until you have them memorized.

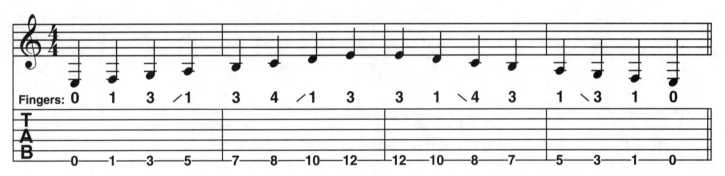

This diagram shows the location of the natural (no sharps or flats) notes on the 5th string. Again, remember that there is a whole step (two frets) between all adjacent natural notes except for "E–F" and "B–C," which are separated by a half step (one fret).

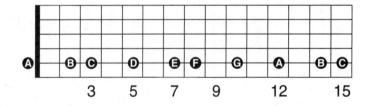

Here are the notes and tablature for the notes on the "A" string. Play these notes until they are memorized.

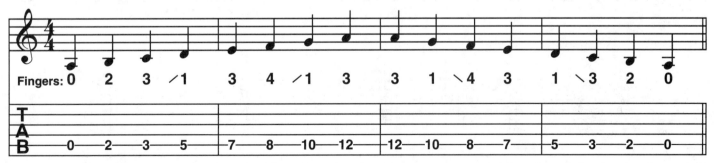

THE "E"-TYPE BARRE CHORD

So far we've only worked on open-position chords. With barre chords, you can leave the open position and play all around the neck.

Barre Chords: A barre chord is a chord in which two or more of the strings are played by one finger laying across those strings forming a "barre."

The most popular type of barre chord is based on the common E chord. To form the barre chord:

1) Re-finger the E chord with your 2nd, 3rd, and 4th fingers.

2) Shift your fingers up one fret.

3) Lay your 1st finger across all six strings at the 1st fret.

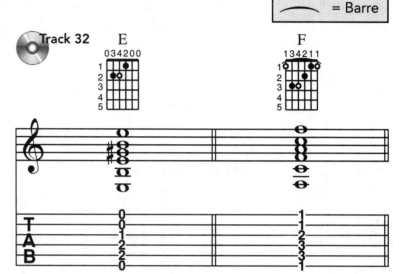

Track 32

$$\frown = \text{Barre}$$

> **Tip:** To add strength to your index finger barre, turn that finger slightly to the side so that the hard, outside edge of the finger forms the barre; not the soft, fleshy part on the inside.

EXAMPLE 16

Track 33

Practice each of the following barre chords. This could be painful at first. Just relax. After a while, you'll get the hang of it.

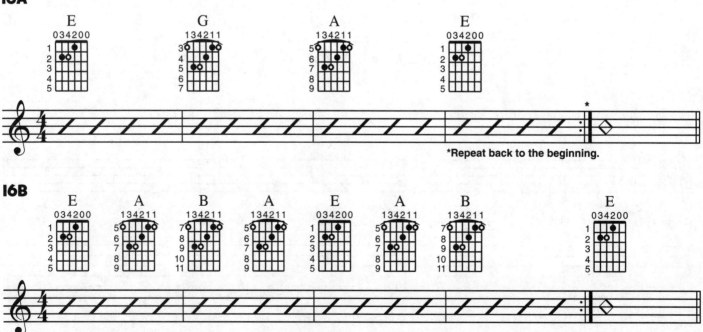

16A

*Repeat back to the beginning.

16B

THE "A"-TYPE BARRE CHORD

The other popular type of barre chord is based on the common A chord. To form the barre chord:

1) Shift your 2nd, 3rd and 4th fingers up one fret.

2) Lay your 1st finger across the top five strings at the 1st fret.

♭ = *Flat.* A flat sign indicates the note is played one fret lower than its natural position.

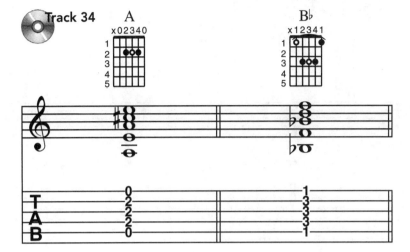

Tip: If it is too difficult for you to play the top string, you can leave it out and play this as a four-note chord. Here is another popular way to finger this type of barre chord: lay the 3rd finger down over strings 2, 3, and 4.

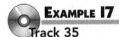 **EXAMPLE 17**

Track 35

This next example uses both types of barre chords.

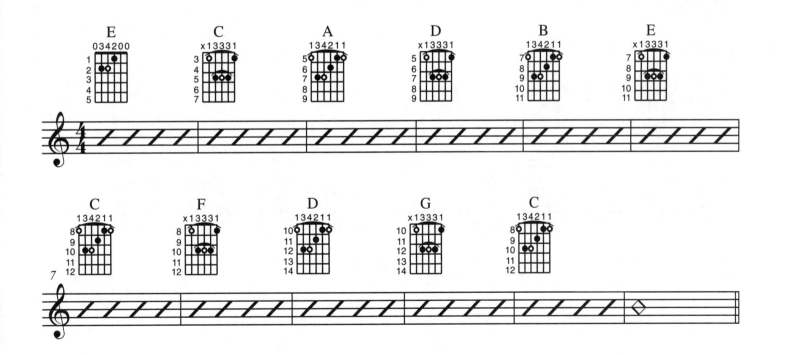

THE "E"-TYPE MINOR BARRE CHORD

Just as you converted the E major chord to an E minor chord by changing one note, you can do the same with the major barre chord.

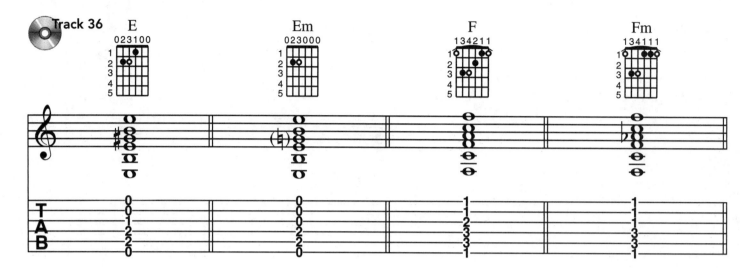

Just as with the major barre chord, the "E" type minor barre chord can be shifted up the neck to any key.

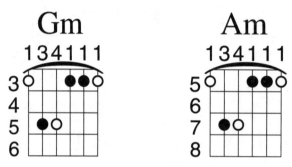

 **EXAMPLE 18**
Track 37

Practice moving between these major and minor "E"-type barre chords.

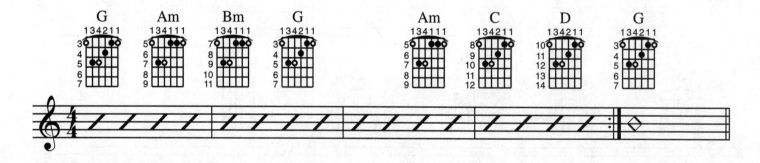

THE "A"-TYPE MINOR BARRE CHORD

Now, let's convert the "A"-type major barre chord to a minor form.

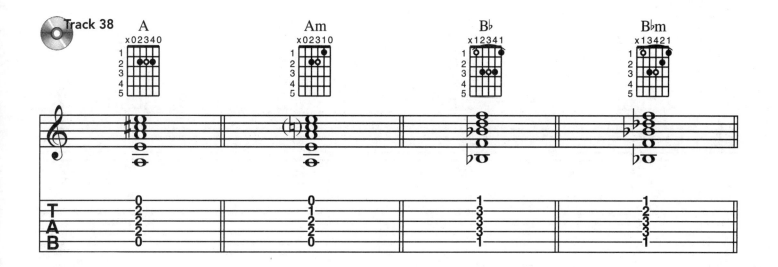

Again, just as in the last example, the "A"-type minor barre chord can be shifted up the neck to any key.

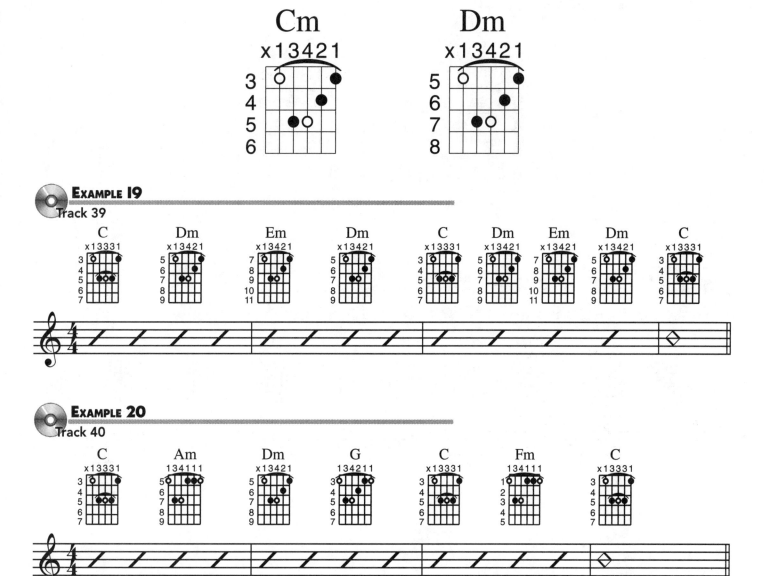

"E"-TYPE DOMINANT BARRE CHORDS

Just as you converted the E major chord to an E7 chord by changing one note, you can do the same with the major barre chord. To play the F7, hold an F barre chord and lift your 4th finger.

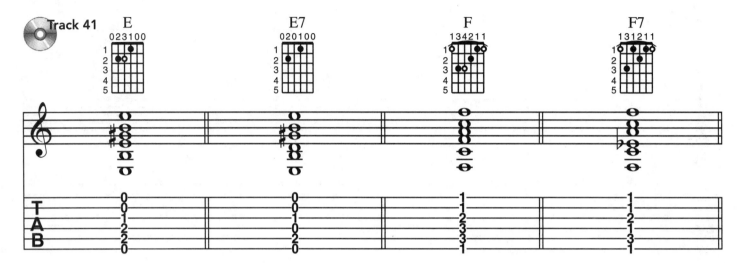

Just as with all the other barre chords, the dominant 7th major barre chord can be shifted up the neck to any key.

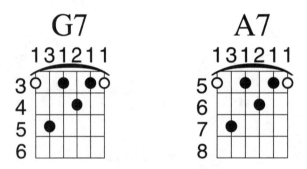

 **EXAMPLE 21**

Track 42

This rock progression uses just dominant 7th chords.

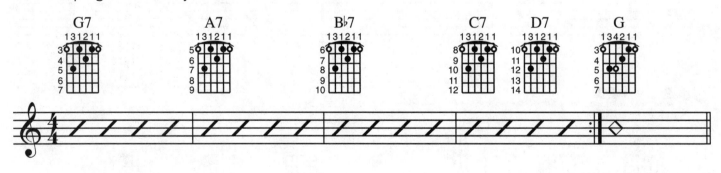

"A"-TYPE DOMINANT BARRE CHORDS

Now, let's convert the "A"-type major barre chord to a dominant 7th form.

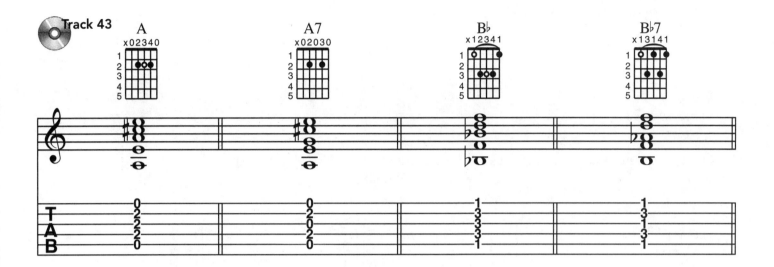

Just as in all the previous examples, the "A"-type dominant 7th barre chord can be shifted up the neck to any key.

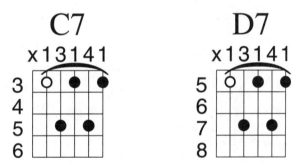

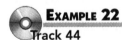 **EXAMPLE 22**
Track 44

This example uses just the "A"-type dominant 7th chord.

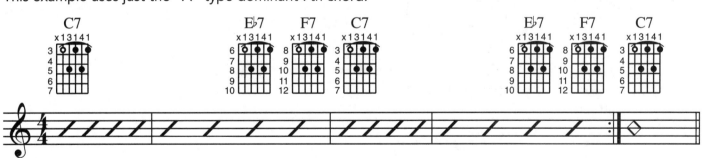

Section Four: Chord Progressions and Strumming

The chord progressions in most songs use combinations of major, minor, and 7th chords. Using just the barre chords you've already learned, you can play the chords to almost any song. Here are a few common chord progressions.

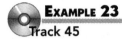
EXAMPLE 23
Track 45

This first progression is one of the most common. In fact, it's probably the single most common chord progression found in old rock and roll ballads.

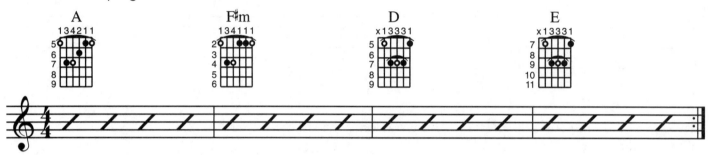

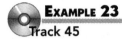
EXAMPLE 24
Track 46

Once you can make the transition from one chord to the next cleanly, try it with this strumming pattern. Maintain a steady down-up motion with your picking hand but only strike the strings where indicated. Listen to the recording to get the feel.

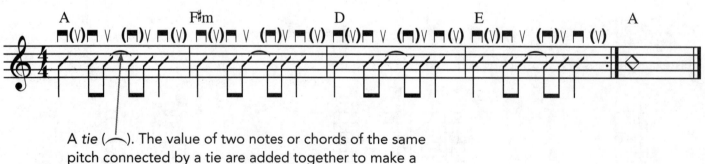

A *tie* (⌒). The value of two notes or chords of the same pitch connected by a tie are added together to make a longer note.

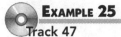 **EXAMPLE 25**

Track 47

This next progression is designed to help you learn your dominant chords.

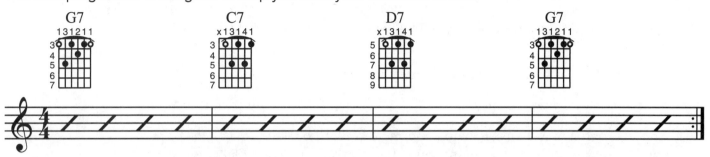

EXAMPLE 26

Now, let's try this chord progression with a new kind of strumming pattern. This pattern uses mostly down-strokes. On the 2nd strum, try *muting* by releasing the left-hand pressure on strings. When you strike the muted strings you produce a short, muffled, slapping sound that adds a very driving, rhythmic effect to your playing. The last strum of the pattern (an up-strum) is also muted. Listen to the recording to get the feel.

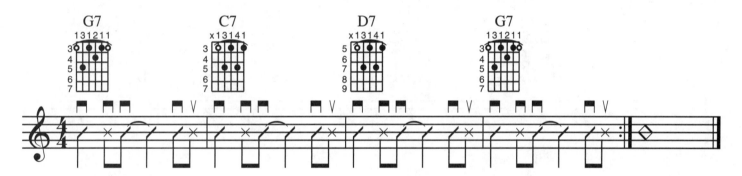

EXAMPLE 27

Track 48

Now put everything you've learned to work in this next challenging chord progression.

- First try playing only major chords for the entire progression. (The major chord forms are shown above the music.)

- After you can play all the chords as major, then try to play only minor chords.

- Next, try only dominant chords.

- Finally, experiment with mixing and matching the chord qualities (major, minor or dominant). See which combinations sound best to your ear. Note: Only the major form of each chord is indicated. Convert these to minor and dominant also.

THE ALL CHORDS PROGRESSION

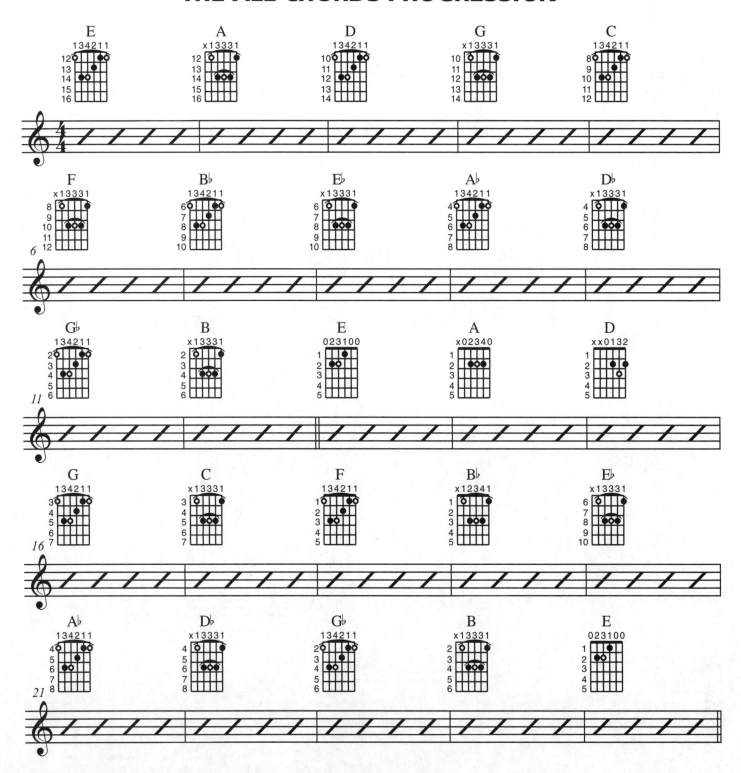

Section Five: Soloing and Picking

Pentatonic scales are found in all types of music, but they are perhaps most commonly associated with blues and rock.

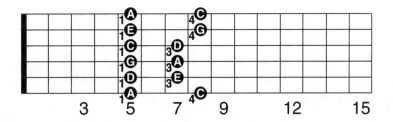

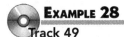
EXAMPLE 28
Track 49

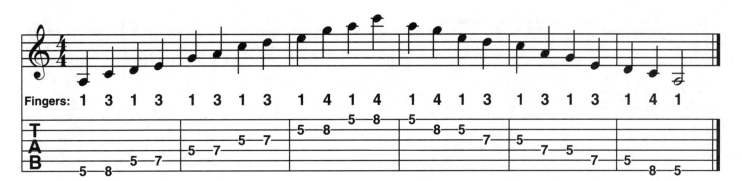

EXAMPLE 29
Track 50

Picking: There are three basic pick techniques:

1. The first is the down-stroke (⊓): Strike the string in a downward motion of the pick.

2. The second technique is the up-stroke (∨): Strike the string with an upward motion of the pick.

3. Alternate Picking: Usually the down- and up-strokes are combined. The up-stroke follows the down-stroke in one smooth motion–strike the string with a down-stroke and then strike the string with an up-stroke as the pick returns to the playing position.

Now play the A minor pentatonic scale with alternate picking.

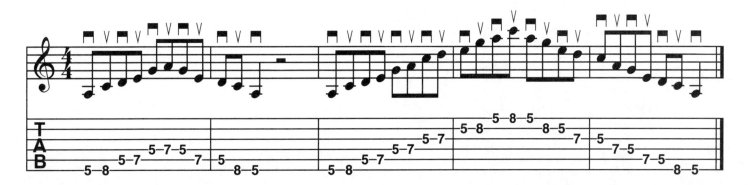

COORDINATION EXERCISES

The most important aspect of developing good picking technique is the coordination of your left and right hands. You must get the pick to strike the string at the exact same instant that the fretting hand is pressing the note down. The following exercises are designed to help you develop good coordination between your left and right hands.

 EXAMPLE 30: THE GROUP OF THREE
Track 51

This first exercise involves playing through the minor pentatonic scale in groups of three. This type of repetitive pattern is called a **sequence**. (Note: the "3" above each each group of notes indicates a *triplet*: three evenly-spaced notes in one beat.)

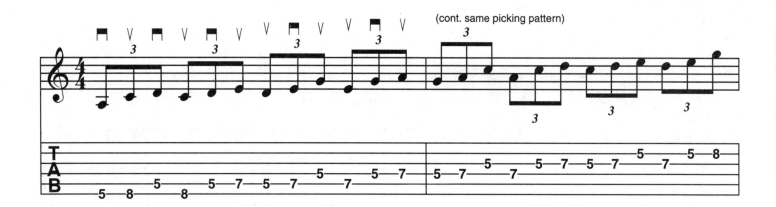

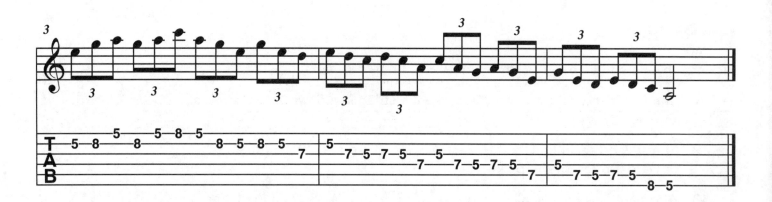

EXAMPLE 31: THE GROUP OF FOUR
Track 52

The next exercise involves playing through the minor pentatonic scale in groups of
four. The tricky part to this pattern is that you often have to use the same left-hand
finger twice in a row. To do this you'll have to roll your fingertip from the first note to
the second.

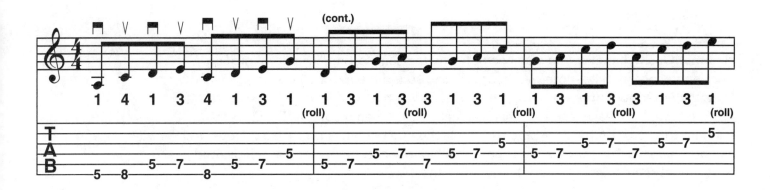

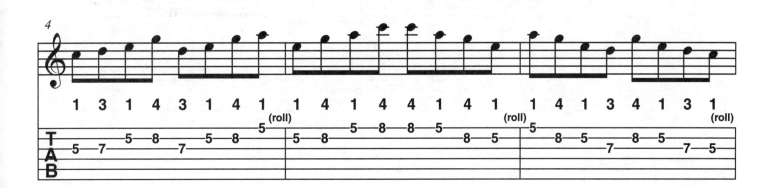

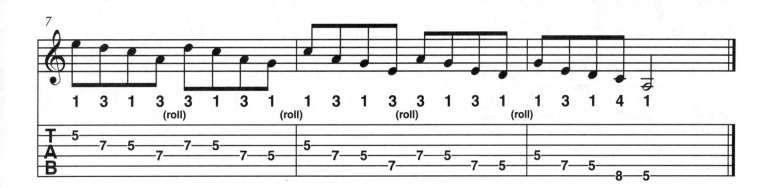

LEAD TECHNIQUES

Track 53

Hammer-ons, *pull-offs*, and *bends* are three of the most important and guitaristic lead techniques to learn. All three of these are *slur techniques*, meaning that they allow you to play more than one note for each pick attack. Slurs give you a smooth, flowing sound. Picking every note tends to sound choppy and mechanical.

HAMMER-ONS AND PULL-OFFS

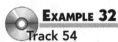

EXAMPLE 32

Track 54

Hammer-Ons: Whenever you play two notes on the same string, instead of picking both notes, play the first note with your pick and sound the second note by "hammering" your finger down onto the neck. The impact of the finger striking the neck is enough to make a sound. This is actually easier than it sounds. Don't try to hammer too hard. With a little practice, this technique becomes pretty easy. Note: You can only hammer "up" from a lower note to a higher note. Each hammer is indicated by a curved *slur* marking in both the notation and TAB.

H = Hammer-on

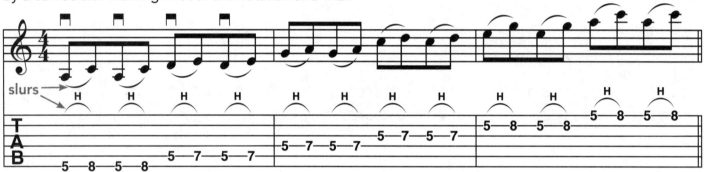

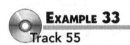

EXAMPLE 33

Track 55

Examples 33A and B are common A minor pentatonic licks that use the hammer-on technique. Try both picking patterns: all down strokes and alternate picking.

EXAMPLE 33A

EXAMPLE 33B

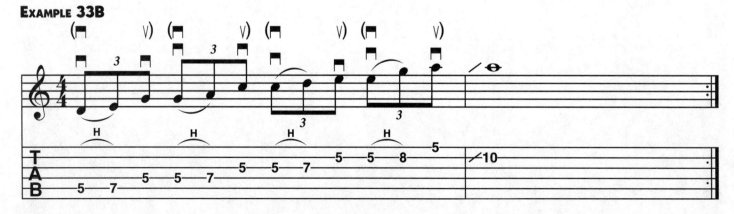

EXAMPLE 34

Track 56

Pull-Offs: A pull-off is the opposite of a hammer-on. For example: Plant your first finger on the 1st string "A" at the 5th fret; now place your fourth finger on "C" at the 8th fret. Sound the "A" by pulling your fourth finger *down* off the string with enough force to sound the "A." Note that both the pull-off and hammer-on are indicated by a curved slur marking. *An upward slur is a hammer-on and a downward slur is a pull-off.*

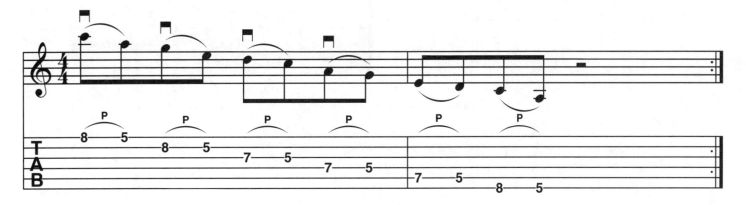

EXAMPLE 35

Track 57

Here's a nice lick in the style of Jimmy Page. Practice this one slowly until you can play it very evenly. Then push it as fast as you can.

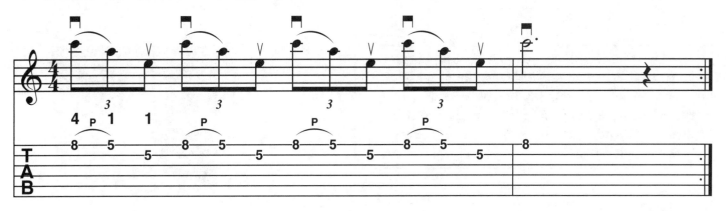

String Bending

 Track 58

String bending is probably the most unique and emotional-sounding technique available to guitarists. Bends are used in all styles of electric guitar playing. When we bend notes we are actually imitating the human voice, which is one of the few other instruments with this ability.

This diagram illustrates the two most commonly bent notes in the minor pentatonic scale.

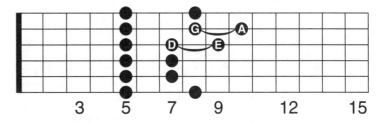

Example 36

First bend the 3rd string "D" up a *whole step* (the equivalent of two frets, e.g. 7th to 9th fret) to "E" (Ex. 36A). This should sound similar to sliding from "D" to "E" (Ex. 36B).

Example 36A

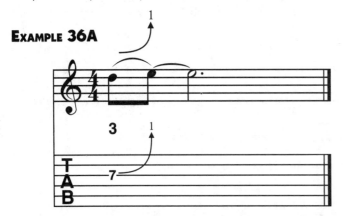

Example 36B

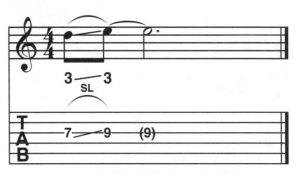

Tip: Don't just bend with your 3rd finger; place your 1st and 2nd fingers on the string also and push with all three. Also, hang your thumb over the top of the neck and bend the string by not only pushing up with your fingers but also by pushing down with the thumb.

Example 37

Try bending the 2nd string "G" up a whole step to "A." You can use either your 3rd or 4th finger on the "G." Either way, support the bend with your remaining fingers. Again, the bend (Ex. 37A) should match the sound of the slide (Ex. 37B).

Example 37A

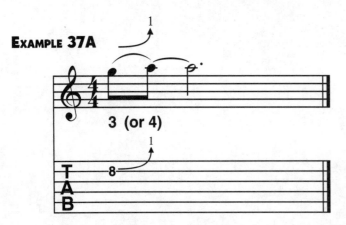

Example 37B

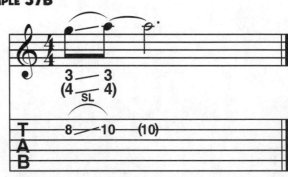

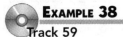

EXAMPLE 38
Track 59

You can also bend a string "down" (towards the floor). This is usually done on a 3rd string bend (the 1st and 2nd strings would get pulled right off the neck).

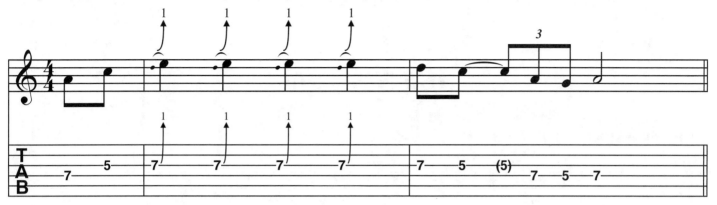

EXAMPLE 39

Another common blues-oriented bend is played with the 1st finger. Try bending the 3rd string "C" a half step (one fret) to "C♯." This is done with the 1st finger pulling down towards the floor.

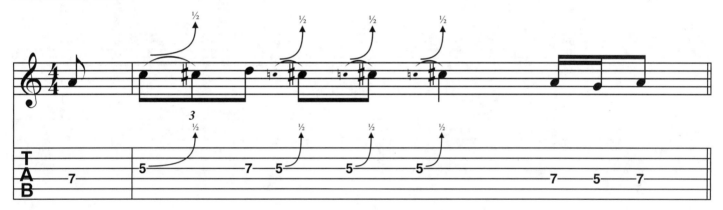

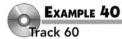

EXAMPLE 40
Track 60

Here's a common lick combining bends, hammers and pulls. The whole thing is derived from the A minor pentatonic scale.

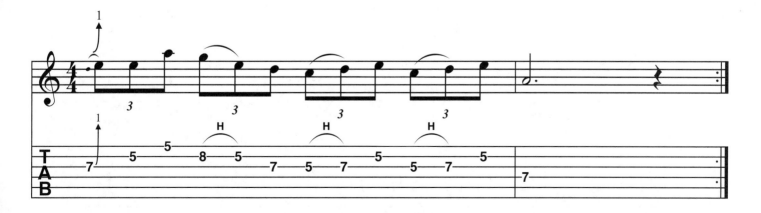

This final jam puts everything you've learned to use. All of the notes are derived from the A minor pentatonic scale. Techniques such as hammer-ons, pull-offs, and bends are applied throughout. Listen to the recording and pick out your favorite licks, then, using the tablature and the notation, practice them until you can play them comfortably. Also, notice the "Blues shuffle" marking; the eighth notes are played unevenly, long-short, long-short.

Often in the blues we bend less than a half step, as in the last note in bar 4, which goes only halfway to the C♯. This is called a *quarter-tone bend*.

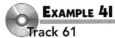 **EXAMPLE 41**
Track 61

THE FINAL JAM

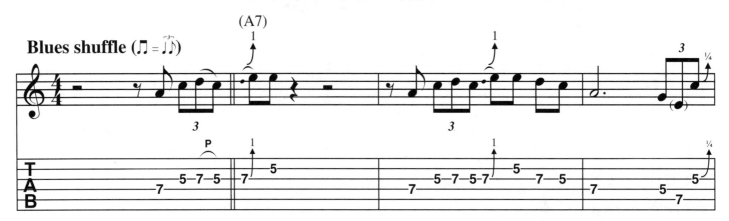

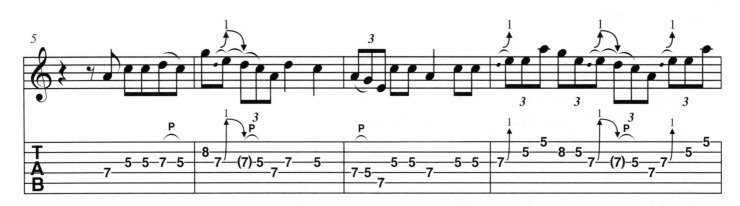

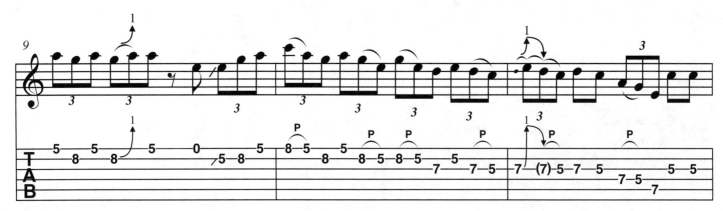

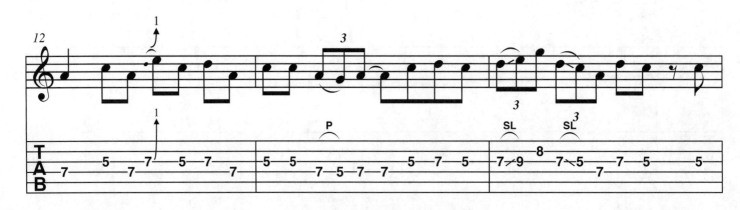

The most important thing in learning to improvise lead is to PLAY A LOT. Here is a blues play-along track in the key of A. Use the A minor pentatonic scale and all of the licks you've learned so far as you improvise to this track.

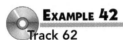

EXAMPLE 42

Track 62

SLOW BLUES JAM

Chord symbols that include a slash mark (A7/G) are called **slash chords**. They indicate a note other than the root is the bass note.

Guitar Chord Chart

OPEN-POSITION CHORDS

A
x02340

Amin
x02310

A7
x02030

B7
x21304

C
x32010

C7
x32410

D
xx0132

Dmin
xx0231

D7
xx0213

E
023100

Emin
023000

E7
020100

F
xx3211

G
210003

G7
320001

BARRE CHORDS

Major
134211

Minor
134111

7th
131211

Major
x12341

(3 3 3)

Minor
x13421

7th
x13141